MY UNCONSCIOUS MIND

My Unconscious Mind

DEMARCUS HOLDER

MY DELUSION

Baby

A mystery of words wrapped together.

intertwined with forces that compete with those of whirlwinds and tornados.

Time has taught me patience and brought me wisdom.

I seek to understand you. Your heart reaches out to me.

your soul wraps around mine in attempt to bond.

Baby I'm broken. Baby I'm no good.

Baby I'm too far gone.

I claim to love you.

I desire to love the way you love me.

Teach me how to love you and how to love us.

The love, the beauty, the scarlet, the fear, the rage that comes with the essence of loves grasp.

We thrived, we blossomed, we flew high, the higher we went the more we dreamed it could last forever.

Love was ours! We had made love! we were the definition of love. I loved you.

I will always love you.

Love ends, love blossoms again.

I relearn to walk and talk love, a love that once came so easily.

Now I choose to love...

Trauma and pain sketched out in different forms.

Our love ripped open, sealed and bonded back together, with a type of hate only a heart break can form.

Mind

Mind is uneven mind is stressed the fuck out.

Mind near gone, no different than my brothers, I've just hid it longer!

Mind was strong mind was beast.

Mind knew love mind knew strength.

Mind slowly fading brain decaying reading to remember.

Mind wants to forget smoking to ease my mind.

Mind is eased by drugs and whiskey sweet whiskey.

Breflection

I see you.
I smell you.
I feel my heartbeat from the innocent arm touches.
I miss you.
Your smile invites me in
Your quietness urges me to protect you.
I dream of you.
I want you.
I need you. I see you.

Reborn

Sleepless nights wrestling myself to sleep.
Bills, Love responsibilities My motivation lacking.
My depression feeds me.
Stress anxiety kills me.
Yet
My motivation stirs.
A newborn babe to keep me eager. A rebirth
Runaway passion rebound.
Everything attached to life now becomes fluid again.

No Title

My mind out of control the thoughts of you destroy me.
I sip another sip, let me never feel the pain of loving you again.
You've hardened me.
You've not only broke me you've cursed me.
I will never love the same again.
Its damn near 2 in the morning yet I sit here writing.
Reminiscing, hating, loving at the same time.
These drinks these sips of whiskey call out to me.
They seemingly heal the pain.
The songs the rhythms they guide my hands my fingers dance on my keyboard to the beat.

Nothing left to say. 08/19/2012

Nothing left to say…
The words I had prepared for you.
Just got erased so I am off to bed…

U know 05/18/2011

Ok I'm not giving up…my tears just show how much I care about you; my pain just shows my weakness…

I swallow gulps of pride my mind yells my head throbs. I feel worthless gave up all I had just to find all I ever wanted was already mine. What do I do now. To die!!

That was years ago, the day they stabbed me so deep, so hard, they took away my heart. to live I never have. from birth I embraced the steel cold bars of this cold world. It's to late, it's out of reach... to gain your love so close yet so far away.

Unwanted is my name. 05/5/2011

I am the unwanted... unwanted is my name... I satisfy the tears of pain.

I satisfy yet am not satisfied more famous than the glorified pope I've cleared my name, a purified soap. when I claim one, I claim them all.

So, listen closely you'll hear my call.

I'll use any and everything to make you understand. Although my brother's name poverty. I count it not, yet I demand.

I've entered many of people's lives, some claim them as their guardian angel protection from all hurt... let's just move on I am unwanted my fate is doom you'll find me at your doorstep soon.

Am I real 5/5/2011

I dreamed a dream the dream felt real I left this world I left my body...

Am I real.

I woke up crying I woke up stiff I woke up dead my soul adrift am I real.

A peace so sweet a peace so swell, what is this a trip to hell. Is this real

Born into a world of hate, woke up sweating drops of blood.

It can't be real.

Lord can't this be my fantasy. Lord erase this from my memory

It is real.

A choice

It shapes my day and molds my night.

It places us ten, 20 years down the road.

Life is real my dreams are true, stop playing Russian roulette with déjà vu.

7-7-1992

On 7-7-1992

Ya that is the day I was born. I entered this world my heart already torn.

Worn out already, no love talks or lullabies. Or maybe from the blunts the crack and her well used bongs. bonded to who?

Nothing but DNA

That's ok for some people. But it messed up my special day.

My mind erased all the memories of pain. But all these... emotions will always be the same. I'm messed up from the inside out. My words don't talk they all scream out. Pain a word I use so often. It probably will be the only word written on my coffin.

Simple as this

A story involving two people who kiss.

A story of two people who wish.

A story of a thing called love.

To most it's still only given from above.

Baby gurl your love is real I cannot speak of it, so I write what I feel. You've brought out all sides of me. You cleared the hate now all I do is see.

You tagged me it I tagged you back now stop and look where we're at. You came to me with hurt and pain your tears fell, those eyes lit with a flame from hell. I knew that you would be mine. I came so close, so I erased the line. I bundled you up inside my arms. I didn't even have to recite any well used charms.

And since that day I've come to see, you and I are meant to be

With my heart I've seen I see. That you and I are meant to be.

Every time we separate my heart feels as if it will break... bundled words yes loose them now. My brain my tongue all said wow.... cus is this real I've seen it before but all of those were forced in doors. You and I a special two... you and I the only two.

You and I are meant to be,

You see... you and I are finally set free! I'm here for you I love you so.

The story of two a special kiss

So grateful we found the love we almost missed so take my hand and keep my heart for us two will never part... I love you.

Saddened with a heart of pain.

Saddened by a cursed, fucking name.

I'll never speak your name again you took my heart and crushed in two ... the only two I've ever loved. My flesh and blood my seed, my name, my legacy. You selfish whore, words don't do justice, words cannot bring the peace I seek.

I cannot find. My holidays now gifted with tears. Gifted with this pain inside... gifted with this life of you!! Saddened by the loss of them.

Saddened now my name is pain.

Stuck

Stuck because of love stuck inside this hate ...living with the thought that this may be my fate…

I move on quick to forgive.

You hung on and drug us through hell. You are stuck inside your mind which makes you narrow it makes you blind… I've had the worst but not like this... it got so bad I hate your kiss. I hate the love we make getting up is hard to fake. Happiness. I try to bring it through my songs I sing.

I sing a tune a tune that tells a different story... that hides this hell. Yet still your stuck inside this place inside your mind away from me you have dug this pit, you tossed me in. I no longer love I lust to sin… when will it end.

When will it go away.

I'm stuck I'm stuck…,

Happiness oct 26/2021

I thought I brought you joy and love. I thought I as your muse... torn apart by childish screams gone off to chase your childhood dreams. Age and death have made a wedge created by the fear they bring. I wish to be loves endless tale. And wish our love would never fail... held together by hope tears wiped away by childlike fears... collide and sway!

sway and collide. let's stay I pray bring back the love and joy once known or let the stars decide our fate.

The last note... 5/21/22

Its over but not over. It never ends but this is the last note, the last words I write. It is but it isn't. Yet I'm letting go.

You control me.

I must let go.

All words have been spoken… you win I give up.

I'll always love you… 1/3/??

Love never dies. Just falls into the dirt and grows into some other form of something… I saw you today red hair flowing. You looked at peace.

I'll never love again echoing in my brain.

I will never love again, i will always love you.

But i will never love again...

We parted ways stepped back and walked away... you know I had to look at that ass one more time… Someone else is loving you.

Someone else is holding you.

Your embrace, that jittery uneasiness... Let's me know your body still wants me.

You kiss my cheek it lets me know you still care. sweet gentle kisses...

I walk away we match each other's stride from isle to isle.

Ill always love you but Ill never love again.

www.ingramcontent.com/pod-product-compliance
Ingram Content Group UK Ltd.
Pitfield, Milton Keynes, MK11 3LW, UK
UKHW031311030225
4420UKWH00050B/1076

9 798218 524593